RAINBOWS IN THE SUN

IN THE SUN

by

Clare Corner

© **Clare Corner**

ISBN 0-9534671-1-2

Published by
The Whole Being Centre Publications
174.Newman Road, Exeter. EX4 1PQ

THE DECISION

Take hold of your courage in both hands
and cup your true feelings within.
Drink from the depths of your nagging doubts
accepting, rejecting at whim.

If you still love her, then tell her so now;
If you don't - let her go - don't be cruel;
for a future in store for a love that's run cold
will only add fire to the fuel.

If there's a voice that tells you to go
ignore it, 'til you are quite sure,
for decisions like these are so hard to make -
it's too late once you've walked 'thro that door.

So when you've examined the rights and the wrongs,
when you've thought through each consequence -
sift 'thro the wheat and the chaff of the grain,
and know your decision makes sense.

Then if the worst happens, and your marriage dies,
Don't fester alone in the dark,
Remember Divine Healing Hands will combine
To guide you towards a fresh start.

FORGIVING

In the beginning was the world
where man learned all his tricks.
He learned to love, to hate, to fight,
to plunder for his kicks.
He learned that on this earth he must
work hard to fill his needs,
For nothing comes of idle hands;
nor food, without the seed.

He learned to recognise his worth
and cultivate his gifts,
Applying lessons learned en-route -
so good, from bad he'd sift.
But in this learning, man could feel
restlessness stir within;
Then avarice led him by the hand
creating power within.

Soon best friend - selfishness - dropped by,
and stayed with man too long;
And very soon lethargy called,
encouraged by man's wrong.
But soon man found he lacked true friends -
no peace-of-mind had he;
Despair was his companion now,
rejection was his plea.

Then one day man cried out for help,
in search of love and light,
He called God's name, time after time,
for rescue from his plight.
God heard man's plea and smiled on him,
with gentle, loving care,
Forgiveness was his gift to man, a quality so rare.

"In loving you," our Father said,
'I take you as you are,
In loving me, hold out your hands
together we'll go far.
Forgive yourself, let go of guilt,
and learn to like yourself;
For that is lesson number one -
a lesson in self-help.

The path of life is paved with thorns,
some sharper than the rest;
Each thorn one of the deadly sins,
not one brings out your best.
Respect the past, learn from it now,
go forward with good grace;
For I have loved you all your life,
I am your smiling face'.

MY PRAYER

*F*ather may I come to you
amidst life's toils and strife?
I need your arms around me now
for guidance throughout life.

I promise, if you care for me,
to place my hands in yours,
I need to know that I can strive
to reach that Open Door.

I know my trembling hands are weak
but you will give them strength;
And if I'm tempted to divert
these hands my fists I'll clench.

I know I chose to suffer now
for Glory yet to come,
I know I am a sinner too,
and have been all life long.

I do believe the time is right
to place my trust in Thee,
You have my love,
you have my faith,
Dear Father walk with me.

I promise I will try to be
all things I know I should;
Humble, loving, patient, kind,
a Keeper of your good.

I had a dream last night you know
in which your healing flowed
into the troubled soul of one
who stood in fear, head bowed.

And in my dream, pulsating fingers
pointed without time;
Those fingers and their palms so hot
I realised, were mine.

Have You I wonder chosen me
to tread the path in life
that helps relieve the suffering
of those who live in strife?

If that is so, dear Father God,
no better gift have I,
For You are the Light that shines in my eyes
and the one who heeds my cry.

ALWAYS

Two blonde heads of innocence
lie curled asleep in bed,
to dream of wonders unforeseen
stored in their tiny heads.

My little boy, my little girl,
all mine, to have, to hold;
two precious reasons for my joy,
two ingots of pure gold.

How deep the bond that binds us close,
unspoken, silent, there -
how great the love I have for you,
how real the joy we share.

One day, my son, you will grow up
to spread your wings and fly
to seek a new life of your own,
forgetting years gone by.

And then, my blonde-haired little girl,
one day you will go, too,
With faltered steps learnt long ago,
and heart of golden hue.

If I can help you, on your way
I promise that I will,
just call my name and I'll be there
supporting, loving still.

And when you're grown, and I am old,
and death knocks at my door,
remember all the love we shared
and let my spirit soar.

COME FLY WITH ME

Fly on the wings of a stallion
breeze on the wings of a dove,
search with the heart of cupid,
live in the realms of love.

Take from life the pleasures,
reject of life the dross,
steadfast hold the Light of One
Who died on a wooden cross.

Reach for the stars in sunlight
hold true love within,
kiss the face of Angels
Bless the truth within.

Search for what is missing
seek and ye shall find,
glory in discovery
bask in truthful mind.

Believe that you are sacred
take not the idle word,
dismiss with love, in truth, in light
wrongdoings you have heard.

Know that He is with you,
Walking by your side,
Lift your heart above your head,
He hears your silent cries.

Fly within your stallion
Soul to Soul are one;
Let no more your fear regress,
Let joy and credence come.

MY SAVIOUR

You are our everlasting peace
our ever-faithful guide,
along this journey dark and drear
beneath Your wings we'll hide.

Oft do we into danger fall
but You are ever near,
to keep us safe and hold us up
in every hour of fear.

You are our ready comforter,
to cheer us on our way;
You will not leave us nor forsake
lest from Your side we stray.

So may we ever faithful be
in this dark world of sin,
and learn to love and cling to you
as on your arm we lean.

THE MAN WITH THE ROSE

𝕴 was given a rose, by a man with a soul
so evolved, I felt humble and proud.
A single red rose, deep claret-rich red,
that stood out like a face in a crowd.

I wondered why he placed the rose in my hands
and ask that I give it to you,
but I trusted his smile, so I took the red rose
with his thanks for all that you do.

Your rose has a name engraved on its' heart,
and a single tearlet of dew;
but the passing of time has strengthened the love
of the man with the rose, for you.

Hold the rose to your heart
and inhale it's perfume,
so vibrant, so sweet, and so pure.
Let it's soft velvet petals envelop your pain,
like the sea would the sand, on the shore.

The man that I saw, came quite close to me
His presence, a joy to behold,
and the Angels beside him, white-feathered of wing,
confirmed what I had been told.

That this special man, touched by God's healing hands
Understands all that you have been through
and he will be there to lift up your heart,
giving strength for the work you must do.

So he gives you this rose, ruby red, claret-rich,
with much love, to have and to hold;
And he wants you to know that your beautiful bloom
is part of God's spiritual fold.

I AM HERE

My precious love, don't mourn for me
or fill your life with pain,
for I can see and hear and touch
and laugh and love again.

I see my photo in its frame
on table, by my chair
I watch you hold it in your arms
and cry 'cos I'm not there.

I am real, as real as you
I haven't gone astray
I've just slipped through God's veil of love
a moments thought away.

I bless your life my darling love,
and hold you constantly,
I've asked God's help to stem the tears
you're shedding still for me.

So call my name out loud, my love
please talk to me again,
and know that I am always here
companion - lover - friend.

SUMMER LOVE

In the misty shadows lurking
'cross the bay of Galway town,
drifting on the morning ether -
soul mates kissing in the dawn.

Loving hearts so tightly blended
'twining thoughts - no need for words;
kindred spirits, urgent , wanting,
feeling, sensing, not just heard.

There across the Bay of Galway
in the dawn of summer love,
stands a man whose heart was captured
flown aloft on wing of dove.

Tall and dark, this magic fellow
bared his heart, his love, his pain;
calling for the lass who loves him
knowing they will meet again.

STANSTED HALL

Weep not for those who stand and wait
when earthly life be done,
hold back your tears of magnitude
for I, too, loved "my son".

I too am crying, with the rain
but my tears give earth life,
for I have sheltered many souls
in search of peace from strife.

I am The Hall, whose chimneys tall
stretch upwards to the sun,
with walls of brick and mellowed vine
and echoes of your fun.

I may be old with tarnished look
and joints that creak with age,
but I too feel, and see and watch
and dread impending age.

Don't take my life into your hands,
nor raise me to the ground,
don't pierce my heart with silent stake
for love interred will drown.

Don't shut my eyes of glassed - paned frames
or doors of polished wood,
for they are also part of me
and by my side they've stood.

So when the winds of change arrive
send out your thoughts and pray,
for I too feel, and sense, and love -
fight hard - and let me stay.

A SECRET PLACE

Underneath your turbulence
where Love is melting strife,
an inner voice - a spirit soul
rejoices in your life.

You are precious in the eyes
of those you cannot see;
their faith, and trust, stand side-by-side,
their message - "You and Thee".

There is a oneness that resides
within a Secret Place,
where fear can sometimes hide behind
the mask that seals a face.

But helping hands are working hard
to chide your spirit on,
and loving arms will fold 'round you
'till all your fears have gone.

So as the hands of time tick by,
have trust and carry on,
for you are precious, my dear child;
and you and Yours, are one.

BROKEN BOTTLES

Take back the keys that you placed next to mine
when you wanted to walk from my life;
I'd like you to place them right next to your own,
forgetting our moment of strife.

You know that I love you in every sense,
with my body, my heart and my being;
so look in the mirror - believe what you see -
a man with a great deal of feeling.

Think of our good times, the moments of caring,
the long nights of loving we've shared;
your eyes of dark navy, mine of pale blue,
reflecting the feelings we've shared.

If, after caring and sharing our lives,
the long months, the weeks and the days,
you feel that freedom is pulling your strings,
then tell me you don't want to stay.

TIMEWARP

I am space on timeless wing
and love cocooned in gold;
I am sunlight spun from dreams
And fairytales untold.

I am spirit clothed in rags
but gilded as the flower;
I am Angel's wings in flight
alight my spiritual bower.

I am voice in silent mode
- instinct on the run;
I am darkness full of light
- moonbeams having fun.

I am timeless consciousness
trapped eternally,
bathed in Knowledge, Truth and Light
- waiting to be freed.

ENIGMA

You are the enigma of starlight
The essence of reality that lives within my dreams.

The sureness of a life so beauteous to come
That Daylight extends her fingers to hold You.

You are the faceless voice I speak to
When uncertainty creeps into my thoughts
And I know not where to turn.

But then I sense You by my side
And in my heart
And I feel You touch me
With courage, and faith, and hope.

You are the voice that lingers
When all is still
And sunbeams stretch in lazy slumber.

You are as sure-footed as daylight drifting to dusk,
And the beauty of Your face makes the
Voice within me reach out to hug Mankind.

How humble I feel in your Presence.

How lucky I am to have found You.

How privileged I feel to have Your love.

16

THE KNOWING

Did you know the child you lost,
Your child who died, still lives.
And do you know just where he is?
Inside the heart that gives.

In disbelief we turn away
when death knocks at our door
Rejecting life as valueless,
rejecting faith once more.

"Why do our children have to die,
Why us, why us" we cry.
"It isn't fair, what have we done,
He didn't say good-bye.

"I cant believe it is a test,
a lesson I must live,
The bad news is, my son is dead.
There's no worse news to give.

Don't tell me time will heal my pain.
It won't, as well I know,
And I don't want to live right now,
I'm angry, LET ME GO."

TOUCHING SOULS

Touch my soul with your soul
sweet Spirit of Life,
teach me Truth, Nature, Light, if you will;
take the hands that I hold out in search of the truth,
and the mind that I'm trying to still.

Help me now in the quiet
to find my own peace;
Peace - that stillness of mind will reveal;
let me glory in Nature and treasure her seed,
then bask in her laughter and zeal.

I know Mother Earth as a sister of mine,
and the oak, mighty oak, as a kin;
for the green of the grass
and the white wing of dove
are a part of Your healing within.

I look to the sky
for the peace that I need,
to the sea, to the sand on the shore,
for all of these things are propellers of thought
but the engine to life is God's door.

Every one of your gifts,
to Man, mortal man -
the daisy, the rose and the swan,
are lessons in life we need to observe,
their beauty was Your ace, you won.

SEARCHING

Two seeds of life,
nurtured by the years,
Breathing, growing,
maturing into adults.

Two seeds of life,
Ripened by the sun,
Weathered by life's storms,
Tossed around in a sea of emotion.

Two seeds of life.
Two adults.
Two children of those seeds.

Two hearts.
Once so loving, now so sad.
Needing to recapture moments past,
Seeking the magnet that drew them together.

DRIFTING SANDS

Please hold my hands and walk with me
down memory lane tonight,
I need to re-live thoughts and dreams
before they fade from sight.

I can't believe you're standing here
beside me, holding hands,
for I have loved you all my life
in spite of drifting sands.

The season's of our life have changed:
three out of four have passed,
but each one special on its own
and each one made to last.

Springtime of life was beautiful
a time of fun and cheer,
a time of growing, finding out
discarding empty fears.

Then summer came - and smiled on us
confirming all we knew
our love was special, glorious,
we knew God's will was true.

Soon autumn knocked upon our door
Gnarled fingers of intent;
With heavy tread and burnished smile
Confirming what was meant.

Now as the winter rears it's head
my darling, we must share
the thought that one day time will take
us forward in God's care.

PERCHANCE TO DREAM

I stood in a garden of loveliness
untouched by human hand,
I tiptoed across pure velvet grass,
greener than any land.

On mythical wing my spirit soared
side-by-side with an angel in white
Where is this place I found in my dreams
and how did I get there that night?

I know there's a world beyond the veil
that is only a whisper away
For I've seen a glimpse of this paradise,
but was not permitted to stay.

I know that our loved ones wait patiently,
for the day we step into their realm
Preparing the moment chosen for us,
and guided by God at the helm.

I strolled down a path of golden hue
In my dream, that special night
and recognised some of the people I saw,
resplendent in glorious light.

'There is no death' was their message to me,
just freedom from fear and pain,
And incredulous joy from being alive
and knowing we'll meet once again.

I turned to the angel in white by my side
Exchanging a smile for a smile,
For I knew it was time to journey back home
And drift back to sleep for a while.

REGRETS

I wish we had spoken before you died,
I wish we had loved once more,
I wish our quarrel had never occurred
But regrets are too late, mon amor.

I prayed to our Father in heaven above
To spare your life purely for me
And that was so selfish for you were in pain
But I was too upset to see.

I wish you could look in my heart just this once,
See the ache that I feel day by day,
feel the pain of it breaking when thinking of you
and I wish you could take that away.

I wish I had been by your side when you died,
kissed your lips in a poignant farewell;
For the pain I am feeling would not now be here,
It's too late, and I'm going through hell.

I pray now the weeks and the months have gone by
that the ache in my heart will soon lift;
and the memories of laughter and love that we shared
will one day make up for our rift.

I know that you loved me as I loved you
and I know that you wanted to stay;
But for reasons unknown, it was not meant to be
and I know you will tell me, one day.

BELIEVE ME

𝕴 come to you with words of love
to mend your broken heart;
I felt I had to come to you,
my message to impart.

You know that death was just a gift
from your world to my own -
it's just a step I had to take,
a Spiritual Light was shown.

I see the face you like to wear
at times when things are hard,
I've felt your pain, with tender love,
and left my calling card.

And yes, I kiss the lips that smile
when tears are trembling near,
I stroke your brow with whispered touch
and I erase your fears.

I've given you a ring of gold
to place upon your hand;
a ring that shines just like our love -
a Spiritual wedding band.

Please take this ring I give to you
and wear it near your heart -
for comfort, hope and peace-of-mind
are gifts it will impart.

Then when the sands of time run out
and death becomes your friend
let go this life and know that soon
your broken heart will mend.

SILVER CORD

Death - you are so beautiful
your face, a fragile smile,
framed tenderly in peace of mind
to free us from our trials.

Death - you are so beautiful
your lacy finger tips
a wedding veil of Light;
a smile on silent lips.

Death, your kiss of burnished gold
reflects the autumn sun,
obscuring chilly winter days
when summer days have gone.

Death, who knocks upon our door
with gentle, loving hands,
help us to walk head high in faith,
towards the Promised Land.

SOMEONE

Somewhere in the darkness
a Light shines bright for you,
that Light is love, that love is God
and He waits there for you.

Somewhere in the darkness
God holds your hands and smiles,
and somewhere in the darkness
His radiance abides.

Somehow in the darkness
you know that you are loved
for healing hands are working hard
ambient from above.

Whenever you feel lonely
or sad, or scared, or low,
remember that light you see
is God's celestial glow.

He loves you dearly, don't you see?
He will not let you down,
nor will He favour others more,
for He's your jewelled crown.

So rest awhile in breathless dream
and love Him while you may,
for Light and Love will walk with you
through every waking day.

DANCING IN THE CLOUDS

I am the love you cannot see,
the perfume, scenting flowers;
crystal gems on sunlit wing -
and fragrant, spiritual bowers.

I'm the stardust of your dreams,
The hope within your heart;
A lovely smile to light your face,
To dry the tears that start.

I'm a whisper in the wind -
a cosmic hand of fate;
The truth behind the silver cord
for those who watch and wait.

I am comfort dressed in rags,
disguised but here to stay,
I'm your guide when you feel lost -
a torch to light your way.

I am dancing in the clouds,
the Face behind your mask,
and I know how you really feel,
all burden, and all task.

Just hold my hands and dance with me,
please - like we did before
for you have been here more than once,
of that I'm very sure.

If you release the hurt inside,
and let your thoughts fly free,
the love you give will be returned,
from whence it came, from me.

MORNING STAR

Somewhere, from the depths of time,
beyond infinity;
Starlight kissed the Light of Love,
To heal and set you free.

Translucent wings of gossamer
soft-touched a morning star;
a star to light your life with hope,
no matter where you are.

FATHER - HERE'S MY HEART

It's dull outside,
The skies are grey,
and heavy with the promise of rain.

It's cold outside,
The wind is tormenting the trees,
and playing havoc with old ladies' skirts.

It's not dull or cold inside my heart though,
It's warm, and glowing, and full of love,
And it belongs unconditionally, to You.

REMEMBERING YOU

Another day, another life,
Another million tears;
Can never, ever, wash away
The love we shared for years.

My darling love, I miss you so,
I miss your touch, your smile,
I miss the essence of your being
I miss you all the while.

I know that you are with me now,
I feel your treasured touch,
I sense your presence here tonight, -
and need you very much.

The roses that you see my love,
Rich, ruby red - are yours,
Each one a tribute to your name,
You've found God's Open Door.

In death, you lived, a joyous birth
progressing in God's Light,
now help me face the loneliness
that crowds my mind at night.

So, on this anniversary,
of death, of birth, of life,
remember that I love you still,
I am your Spiritual wife.

THE DANDELION SEED

Are you the embryo I lost,
the soul I never bore?
The product of my bleeding womb
the child I never saw?

I watched you drift in midday sun,
alone, on feathered wing,
a fragile seed, a parachute,
with joyous song to sing.

You floated past my tear-stained eyes,
with gentle manner born,
I sensed you came with some intent -
a re-incarnate born?

You brushed my cheek with tender touch
with soft all-knowing ease,
as sunlight kissed your fingertips
and danced with golden breeze.

Perhaps you're not the seed that floats
to Mother Nature's soil,
maybe you live beyond the Veil
quite free of earthbound toil.

It doesn't matter where you are,
or what or how you live,
my love for you will never die
I have so much to give.

I ache to feel your little arms
nestled close to my breast,
but that was never meant to be
I know that was God's test.

So if you are that dandelion
so pure in spirit gold,
come kiss my cheek this time next year
I'll know it's me you hold.

SPIRIT OF GARA

𝕿empestuous is the sea of life crashing to the shore
foaming waves of silver white, knocking Gara's door;
selfless is the love within, for all the world to see,
luminosity of life, setting whole self free.

Steadfast are the thoughts strong held within a Sacred Cross
joyously the Light and Love, melting mournful dross;
reaching out in Godly love, descending spiritual bowers
taking hold, losing not - sunlit silvery showers.

Taking love, stretching long across a wide ravine,
nurturing the Golden Light, residing to be seen;
knowing Angels flock beside, shoulders stooped in sorrow
holding steadfast faith within, believing in tomorrow.

Looking to the silent night where moon and stars combine
seeking light reviled no more - letting spirit shine;
knowing God sheds tears with us; laughs with joy, with glee;
search no more that candle flame - BELIEVE that you are free.

AN ANGEL KISSED ME

My nightmare was reality;
Cancer was my foe.
I couldn't come to terms with it
And prayed for it to go.

In desperation I lashed out
At those who loved me most,
"Where is my Guardian Angel now?"
I wondered, without boast.

I didn't have too long to wait,
for in my dreams one night
a voice, serene with hope and love,
spoke to me, with foresight.

"Give me your hands" an Angel smiled
and feel the strength I give;
The strength to cope, the strength to pray
the strength to fight, and live.

The day that you found out the truth
(Your cancer was die-cast)
- that black and panic-stricken day,

a million seconds passed.
I felt your anger, and your tears
as though they were my own.
I saw your look of disbelief
and tried to take it home.

But when I reached that Open Door
God beckoned me to him,
enfolding me in Love and Light
Serenely, from within.

His healing hands now work with you
to fight dis-ease, and win,
for you've been given much spiritual strength,
Now YOU have faith in Him.

The power of prayer is very strong
and it will help you through:
God's spiritual love is yours to keep,
Believe it, 'cos it's true."

"I now believe I've seen God's Light
I've felt His Power within
I'm GOING TO FIGHT - I'm GOING TO COPE,
I'm GOING TO LIVE, AND WIN!"

FLOWERS IN MY GARDEN

Spirit realms are beckoning
a far and distant land,
showering thoughts of yesteryear
revealed by slight of hand.

But conflict etches deep and long
the mind whose thoughts they fill,
for the struggle is, what, where, when, why,
and the dream I have lies still.

Along the lone and winding road
the buds of life appear,
and Mother Earth's vibrating life
is proof that God is near.

SONG OF INNER LIGHT

O inner Light perpetual,
shine in my darkest deep,
illumine step by step the path
for my poor stumbling feet.

Through mountain pass, by precipice,
across the desert track,
when sinks the sun that lights this world
shine brighter through the black.

And when the moon withholds her light,
or clouds blot out the stars,
O Inner Light shine brightest then,
through night's most lonely hours.

Then as I near the river's ford,
that hour before the dawn,
in that the darkest hour of life,
shine as the sun at morn.

With Thee within, O Inner Light,
shining with mystic ray,
my heart shall sing each step I take,
within eternal day.

A TIME FOR PEACE

I was handed a garland of spiritual flowers
by a man I couldn't see,
He appeared as a vision of brilliant white
and he came with a message for me.

I give you this garland - your life - my dear
the stranger said with a smile,
each flower is linked by a stem of love
plucked from my spiritual bower.

I'd like you to cherish each bloom if you will
and inhale life's pure fragrance within,
for the essence of love is contained in each bud
and bonded by friendship therein.

The flowers you see are of spiritual hue
Lilacs, pinks, purples and blue;
each colour a reason, a lesson in life
to be learned, and accepted by you.

I know there are times when life's lessons seem cruel
and your journey through life hard to bear,
but remember, I walk hand-in hand with you, too
now - rest safe, and know I am there.

So, I give you this garland of flowers with my love
and I give it in peace and with joy,
As an angel once said, of a gift he too, gave,
To Mary - her baby boy.

SPIRIT IN THE WIND

You are the breeze that ruffles my hair
and warm sunshine ripening corn;
You are soft rain, caressing the trees,
and the beauty of bird song at dawn.

You are a counterpane of crisp leaves
and the rustle of footsteps on snow,
you are the droplets of dew on a web
spun by spiders - diligent; slow.

You are the solace we pray for at night
when our worries seem larger than life;
And you are the feeling of instinct we have
when we know a decision is right.

You are the flight of peace to our hearts -
a journey of healing kind;
opening windows, revealing your light;
unlocking closed doors in our mind.

You are the echo I hear in the wind -
Compassionate, full of pure love,
nurturing man with wisdom and truth
carried high on the wings of a dove.

So Spirit of Life may I walk close to you
hand-in-hand, side-by-side with your smile;
and Spirit of Peace may I sleep in your arms,
wrapped in heavenly cloak for a while.

THE PHONE CALL

"Hello? HELLO?!! "Are you there, God? Good, 'cos I'm ringing to tell you I can't take any more.

If this is another lesson for me to learn it'll just have to wait until I've picked myself up, dusted myself down and got ready to accept another smack in the mouth. I know You're testing me, but how much am I expected to take before I see a glimmer of light on the horizon?

No - I'm not feeling sorry for myself. Allright, well, yes I am and I'm angry - at me, at You, at the whole flipping world.

WHY? Because I know full well you're going to load my shoulders with as much as You know I can cope with, and I know You're watching me, observing my mistakes and smiling.

OK - I know you're trying to lift my spirits, and I know You're not laughing at me, but I don't want to do this, God - I really don't.

'Pardon? Me? Nah! I don't believe you! Why would I choose to go through all this stuff? PARDON?

I thought I was trying. I thought I was coping as best I could even though my best IS a bit shaky at times. OK, I will keep on trying.

Well, could we do a bit of compromising then? Could you please shine Your torch just one step in front of me from time to time so I

38

can see where I am going?

Oh. You do already. Uhuh! You see, sometimes I feel completely disorientated; it's as though I've been riding on a carousel and lost my sense of direction when I get off. Do You know what I mean, God?

I really do love You, you know. I know it's not your fault I fall back three steps to one forward, sometimes. And I don't mind really, it's just that because You live within me, You know me better than I know myself - I think, if You get my drift.

I know. But all that matters to me is that somewhere along the way I can help make someone smile, even for a minute. You know how it is.

So God, I'm going to try harder to accept my 'fate' with humility and love, and I'll fight the good fight until You say "Yes - you'll do!".

Pardon me? Oh! My name's Clare!!

A TIME TO KNOW

𝔄s you seek the Light
seek also God's help;
for surely shall you find it
within your own temple of the Spirit.

Rejoice in His Love - a love that calms your fears,
dries your eyes, supports and heals you;
lessens your pain and walks always, beside you.

Love God the Father
For in loving Him, all your needs are met.
There shall be no need for worry
For Faith, Hope and Charity is Thy Name.

Seek only the living flame that grows within.
That Light shall be you, and you WILL go forth
emerging as a butterfly with wings of gossamer
perched on life's rays.

Search only for that which can help others free
themselves from bondage; for surely will they also
see God's Light - and yet ANOTHER seed will have
become embedded in the heart of man.

Only then can you heal yourself.
Accept God into your life and
His Love into your heart.

Rejoice in the companionship of His Spirit
incarnate and discarnate. Cherish love in one another.
Know that you are never alone, for God walks with you.

Let His compassion
be a handkerchief for your tears,
and His smile
the sunshine in your life.

SHADES OF AMBER

I love you, I love you, I honestly love you,
let the mask of your fears slip away,
take the love that I give, hold it tight in both hands
and remember my love in the rain.

Take my hands in your hands and feel all my strength,
know the oak, mighty oak, loves you too;
take the green from it's leaves and the brown from it's bark
and bask in the healing you feel.

Take the minutes of life ticking by in the wind
as they search and confirm what you know,
that the clock of your mind is telling the time
and the second hand now points to go.

Imagine my face in the lone, lonely nights,
watch me search for your face and then smile;
it's time, and it's happened, the pretence has now gone,
and our love has cemented the while.

Take and give, give and take, for my life can be yours
to enjoy, to blend with, to savour;
and I will be there, in the cool dawn of day,
relinquishing past-life behaviour.

My spiritual pen, held in hot burning hands,
brings you healing of amber and blue,
and the image of you, held so close to my heart
reflects love, unconditional, true.

In a world ever changing, in search of the truth,
we stray long and hard from our path,
but the path I now tread, is so clear, and ahead
that I know I've accepted my wrath.

If I ever hurt you in deed, or by word,
sift the wheat from the chaff, just for me;
then together, harmonious, hand-in-hand, side-by-side,
we'll march forward through life, chattel free.

WHO OR WHAT

I see you in the morning
When dawn peeps through the night,
I see you in the noon - time
When the sun greets birds in flight.

I see you on the brink of dusk
where shadows long to play,
I see you each and every hour
transposed on earth to stay.

I see you paint the flowers each morn
with brush of rainbow hue,
dipped gently in your spiritual bowl
of pinks, lilacs and blue.

I watch your smile melt icicles
upon a wintry bough,
I see a snowdrop push it's way
throughout the frozen ground.

I see the trees acknowledge you
with swift and gentle nod,
as soft you kiss their fingertips
and melt the frozen sod.

I see you balanced on a web
of gossamer and lace,
a crystal dewdrop looking glass
a mirror for your face.

But then I saw you inside Man,
the hope of future years,
a word of comfort for the lost,
a handkerchief for tears.

I saw you take a faithless soul
and breathe fresh life within
then watch the faltering steps man took
to wash away all sin.

And in my looking I did see
with astral eye in flight,
divinity of sacred thought
forever in my sight.

FLOSSY

𝕱eline grace that held us spellbound sure. Gentle, persistent cries when needs for love abound. That loving stare when on our lap she meant to be no matter what we thought! A purr, a pummel a lick - then rotation, till she found her niche in our arms as a baby nuzzles it's mother's breast. A contented peek through half-closed eyes as if to say, 'now I'm happy, so I'll sleep!' No need for words, just glances in those feline eyes spoke volumes for the mutual love we shared. She knew, we knew, what game and when she'd play, knowing full well she'd get her own way in the end.

But then she died - victim of circumstance and car, leaving us bereft, unable to accept her death without fare-well. Our darling Flossy, gone but in transition; fur still soft and warm beneath our angry tears of disbelief.

> Then one night she came to me
> in dream state, fit and well
> to say good-bye (there was no time)
> and bid me fond farewell.
>
> Her eyes shone brightly, full of love
> for me who missed her so,
> but in that moment, comforted,
> I knew she had to go.
>
> She waited till I cuddled her
> and kissed her soft white fur,
> and whispered softly words of love
> that both of us would share.
>
> All at once she struggled free,
> from arms that held her tight,
> with backward glance, she disappeared,
> as softly as the night.

OPPOSITE

I am soft rain caressing the trees;
you are the sun, on bended knee,
I am the snow glistening white,
you are Jack Frost in dead of night.

I am a woman, struggling for life,
you are a man, emotions rife;
I am a person in my own right,
you are the shadow, concealing my light.

I am the arrow that makes you bleed,
you are the bow, releasing that need,
you were my partner until I said no,
I am free spirit, I had to go.

PROMISE ME

When days are too dark and nights are too long
and the pain in your heart stops you sleeping,
remember that I feel the same way as you,
and I can't get MY heart to stop weeping.

When the chill winter winds and the bare-leaved trees
wrap their snow-laden arms around yours
feel the warmth of my smile melt the ice in your heart
for I'm the Effect, you're the Cause.

I promise I'll stay by your side right though your life
to guide you and to guard you, where the need,
for the path that you must tread in order to progress
is thorny and uneven and crude.

If you look inside yourself with no thought of praise or blame
the face behind the mask will soon reveal,
a prism of your life become a full-blown dream
so the wounds that you have suffered can now heal.

Take the hope that floats on a white fluffy cloud
and God's love and trust in you, in your hands.
Feel the strength of a rainbow - it will fill your pot of gold
as you strive to walk towards the Promised Land.

TOUCH ME

Ethereal fingertips seeking to touch;
emaciate souls aquiver;
prevailing destiny, roof-top aloft;
blockages, stemming life's river.

Qualms of the present, calmed by the
chaste-running waters pervading the mind;
seek not a reason, stilling the now;
chase not the ties that bind.

Purge from the soul - that holding back;
cherish now; spiritual seed;
mind-dance as one, intuitive thought;
confirming reverent creed.

MY SON

Thank you my son for the light in my eyes
That reflects so much love there for you;
And thank you my son for loving me
In a way only known by we two.

Thank you, young man, for the pleasure you give
to a mum growing older in years;
and the memories I have of you growing up,
in spite of torn trousers and tears.

Remember the times that you couldn't sleep
for reasons known only to you?
So I'd sit on your bed, and read you a book,
or make up a story for you.

And when you felt poorly, with childhood ills.
I'd stay by your side through the night;
and rock you to sleep in my arms for a while
'till your tears dried and faded from sight.

Now you're a man and you have your own life,
and it's right that this should be so,
but the tears we have blended for that which has passed
may take quite a long time to go.

I wish you could look in my heart just this once
- see the guilt that I feel day by day,
just knowing your heartstrings broke 'cos of me,
and I wish I could heal them some way.

I want you to know that I left home, not you,
and one day I hope you will find
that life is worth living, that you will feel good,
and even enjoy peace of mind.

So as the dusk whispers that night's on its way,
and the rest of the world goes to sleep,
I want you to feel the strength of my love,
'cos it's yours darling, always to keep.

WHISPERS IN THE WIND

Mummy, Daddy, look within
Your hearts and hear my voice;
You know I didn't want to die,
But it was not my choice.

God felt my pain and saw my tears
He thought, and then He said
That I should hold Him by the hand
And feel His love instead.

I felt soft peace come over me,
And drifted off to sleep -
I saw an Angel with white wings
Prepare my soul to keep.

God's carried me to Heaven with Him
Where all His children stay,
My new home's called the Summerland,
And it's from here I pray.

Mummy, Daddy please don't cry,
Or fill your life with pain,
For I can see, and hear, and touch,
And laugh and play, again.

I'm still the child you loved so much,
It's just that I'm not there.
But I do hug you in your dreams,
And tell you I still care.

Please Mummy, Daddy talk to me,
'Cos I still hold you tight,
And even though you're not aware,
I'm with you - every night.

GLOBAL WARNING

Water that trickles merrily
Over the tombstones of life.

Cascading streams of unmitigated love.

Penance poison inflicting
Misery within our souls.

Cascading gems of crystalline music.

Trees of thought bowing swiftly
In reverence to the sun.

Moon chakras knowing all;
Waiting for the listening ear of mankind,
Knowing he will reject what he sees
Because he is afraid of his destiny
Even though he knows what is to come.

Your earth will self-destruct
Unless you listen to our word.
Why can't you understand what we say
When we speak in your tongue?

Are you unable to hear - those of you we speak to?
Impending doom will not wait forever.
Even now, it is on its way.

THIS IS A GLOBAL WARNING.

Tides will swell.
Rivers will flood.
The earth-plane will break open into craters.

Many will die.
Many will be saved.
Trees will disappear.
Plant life will shrivel.
The sky will open to blackness
The sun will not shine anymore.

The sea will rise.

It will be very cold upon your earth.

PEACE BE WITH YOU.

HOLDING ON

Sometimes, in life, we must let go
of things that cause us pain,
sometimes in life the ones we love
use us for their own gain;
sometimes in life our loved ones die;
perhaps a marriage ends;
and maybe, sometimes, we feel lost,
in spite of prayers we send.

If we see a glorious rose,
sweet-scented, vibrant, pure,
or watch the flight of fledgling birds
upon a distant shore
or if we catch the smile of one
whose love we want to share,
we try to keep those memories, forever in our
care.

We try sometimes to capture moments
that have long been lost
wishing we could keep them safe
in some Pandora's box.
But memories are part of us,
whatever we may feel,
and only we can nurture them,
nourished by God's zeal.

We must hold on to every thing
we treasure in this life
and make the most of all we have,
in spite of toils and strife.
And in this holding on to faith,
and trust and love and hope.
We must believe that our dear Lord
will help us all to cope.

For I believe He lives within
the heart of all mankind,
it's up to us to 'go within'
in search of what we'll find.
Don't ever think that you're alone,
that no-one has the key
to unlock all your grief and pain,
for God can set you free.

For He will always cherish you
with love that knows no bounds,
So listen to that voice within,
to all those spiritual sounds
Hold on to all your hopes and dreams,
forever and a day
'Cos they are precious things to have,
don't let then fade away.

TELL ME

Tell me this is not a dream,
that I'm awake and here;
tell me words you softly spoke
as then you held me near.

Tell me how to ease the pain
of loving you too much -
that time has not erased the thoughts
that long to stay in touch.

Tell me how to live my life
when all the hope has gone,
when crystal teardrops maim my face
where kisses once rained on.

Tell me that the pain you feel
for moments shared and lost
will be replaced by loving arms
no matter what the cost.

Then one day, when the hands of time
embrace first you, then me,
remember moments shared, my love,
and kiss the heart that's free.

LOSING A CHILD

Love the child that holds your hand,
Dear Father - 'cos he's mine,
cherish him and watch him grow
from boy to man, sublime.

Please tell my baby why he died,
that it was meant to be,
that he has so much work to do,
before he comes for me.

Because he passed before his birth,
I didn't say good-bye;
How could I know he had a soul?
I only knew to cry.

Please take this love I give to you
and share it with my son,
call him by his spiritual name,
and love his sense of fun.

I have a message for my child,
although he's gone from sight,
but I will speak with him myself,
by thought, in sleep, tonight.

'Cos when I close my eyes to dream,
and see him standing there
my heart just glows with love and pride,
what better gift to share?

In the stillness of this night
I'm going to tell my son,
I'll love him till the end of time,
'till time on earth be done.

LIVING YOUR DREAM

Have you a dream concealed in your heart
that no-one but you knows is there?
And have you a dream, held tight in both hands
to be cherished, and nurtured and shared?

Have you a dream, so precious - like gold
that to keep it would make you a king?
And have you a dream, no riches can buy
for its wealth is time - travelled on wing?

Dreams are God given, the reasons for why
only we as recipients can know,
But they are the seeds of hope in our lives
from acorns to mighty oaks grow!

I have a dream that mankind will unite
invoking a prayer so intense
That a mantle of reason descend on this world
compensating for man's lack of sense.

Mankind is determined - creating his doom,
for nothing but personal gain,
ignoring the pleas of we far-seeing few
to preserve this old world; not to maim.

We as mere mortals are here on this plane
to learn, to experience, then grow,
but how are we going to feed Mother Earth
if the seeds of God's wisdom aren't sown?

We should value the air that keeps us alive,
we should treasure the trees that give wood,
for the efforts we make in the time that we have
will reap harvests for our children's good.

So when the dusk whispers that night's on its way,
and the rest of the world falls asleep,
remember God's harvest of life could be yours,
and that's a vast ransom to keep.

WISHING

If I could have one wish this night
delivered by moonbeam,
I'd ask for you to hold me tight -
to hug me whilst I dream.

And in my dream, my special dream
my wishes would unfurl,
and we would hold each other close,
encased like oyster pearl.

And you would tell me how you felt
and I would sense your pain,
inflicted by the sword of death
for feelings that could maim.

And in my dream I'd heal your wounds,
and kiss your hurt good-bye,
and you would smile your lovely smile,
no more the need to cry.

For you're a special man, my love
with so much love to give,
a man who knows a woman's needs,
a caring sensitive.

And when I woke, I'd see you there
arms round my curled-up form;
and we would sleep in blissful peace
from twilight hours 'til morn.

REACHING OUT

Somewhere, some place, some corner street
A child in need screams loud;
His hands, outstretched in search of hope
Are thin, but he's not proud.

Those silent screams are loud and clear
Perched on life's window-sill
But that small child knows not the way,
He's lost, and crying still.

His needs are written on his face
Etched deep on furrowed brow,
He needs a lifeline of his own,
He needs it soon, like NOW.

Can we, who give our children life,
Reach out with selfless heart,
To cherish, care, protect, provide, -
To give that child a start?

Let's recognise their spiritual needs,
Let's nurture Love's pure seed,
Let's fill those aching hearts with hope
By thought, by word, or deed.

We know the power of prayer is strong,
So let's unite and pray,
That every child in need survives
To tell another tale.

Our children are tomorrows dream,
They are the vat of life,
Let's fill that empty vat with love,
And help them in their strife.

USER OF DREAMS

Time and space and travelled wing,
and cowboy boots of old,
remind me of the times we shared
and how my pride was sold.

Distant memory takes its toll
on those who cannot stay,
and those that are the residue
get on their knees and pray

I prayed thank God I saw the light
for how and what you are,
no more the wondering when you'll call
no more the wandering star.

But broken bottles cannot cry,
just jagged teeth have they,
just voided space where time stands still
and brush to sweep away.

I bear the toll for all the tears
I've cried thro' sleepless nights,
I've coped the best I can till now,
now I don't want to fight.

Take me on wings to distant shores
where pain will not exist,
where I can sleep in loving arms
where I will not be missed.

And if God's healing hands are real
get them to work on me,
inject into my abscessed heart
numbness, to set me free.

FREEDOM

How do I tell you I'm going to leave
for a land where the sun always shines?
How do I tell you I have to go soon
that the choice to stay here isn't mine.

How can I tell you I want to be free,
that my body and soul yearn for peace;
that if you still love me as I love you,
let me go with a love that won't cease.

I didn't know how to tell you that I
Am very soon going to die,
that freedom from torment is winning the race,
that freedom from pain is my prize.

I want you to know that I'll love you always -
and I'm sorry to die quite so soon,
but I am at peace, with God at my side,
so prolonging my pain is no boon.

Thank you for caring, and sharing my life,
for making me feel I belong,
for cherishing moments shared through the years,
and teaching me right from wrong.

In death as in life, I will treasure your love,
remembering you as you are,
I'll think of the good times, forgetting the bad,
then I'll kiss your sweet lips with my smile.

LONELINESS

Yours is the name I whisper out loud
when the rest of the world falls asleep;
mine's the solitude, I strive to endure
when I am alone with my grief

In the shadows on walls I see your face,
unmarked by the passage of time;
on the bedroom door, your silhouette,
clear-cut - unblurred - in your prime.

I walk up the stairs and hear you call
my name, out loud I think;
I turn in relief to love you once more
but you've gone and I've lost the link.

I do miss that old familiar smile -
comforting, like well worn shoe,
I miss the feel of your arms around mine,
and I miss the essence of you.

Sometimes, I think I can feel your touch,
very gentle, very brief, very real,
a moment of healing, given by God,
easing the pain I still feel.

I know that you loved me as I love you
and I know that you wanted to stay,
but for reasons unknown it was not meant to be
and I know you will tell me one day.

I'LL WALK WITH DREAMS

𝕴'll walk with dreams.
I will no longer go fired by the sun
or frozen by the moon,
swung on the rushing wings of joy
I know that grief drags at those pinions over-soon.

I'll walk with dreams - I will no longer heed
Your beauty, delicate and proud as snow;
You are an arrow that could make me bleed
Were I to bend my body to your bow.

I'll walk with dreams.
These have no shape or touch,
No anguish to wound me overmuch.

A DIFFERENT CHRISTMAS MESSAGE

While shepherds watched their flocks by night all seated on the ground
discarnate spirit gathered near and glory shone around!
The message came clairaudiently in loud, familiar voice
and woke those sleeping in the pews - they had no say or choice.

The medium sensed clairsentiently, fragrant perfumed bowers
then heard the rattling of a box and saw some spiritual flowers.
She saw a lady standing tall, so strong and free from pain
beside her stood a white-haired man of high repute and name.

Clairvoyantly she saw them smile and nod in cheerful glee
they had the best deal after all and their mince pies were free!
The medium's evidence was good. Now! Why had they drawn near?
To celebrate a special time of love and spiritual cheer?

Their message came in unison " we know the strife within -
Unite in love, not daggers drawn, then watch the dream begin.
We love you all who stand and serve in thought, by word or deed,
Hold out your arms and don't let down, your fellow man in need.

Then silence reigned - the medium smiled - she knew her job was done.
For when she gazed around the Church a spiritual light had shone.
The link then faded but two names came quickly to the fore
And as she gave them off we all escaped through the back door!!

(In loving memory of Lillian Hunt and Gordon Higginson!)

TOO LATE

I searched my friend's face to discover the truth
but her tired eyes were brimful of tears,
her waiting was over, the time had now to come,
for to rationalise all her fears.

She stretched out her arms, so weary and and tired,
in her quest to find hope one more time.
I could see that her mask of pretence had now slipped,
and I wished all her anguish was mine.

"I'm dying, Clare" were the words that she used,
quite simply, no tremble in voice.
"Please give me some healing for my peace of mind"
I knew she was speaking the truth.

I held out the hands that were clasped in my own
and I knew God was right there with me
together we gave her the love from our hearts
knowing her tired soul would be free.

MUST I?

Must I from dreams awaken to a dream
and think I see your presence on the air?
Sharper than reality it seems -
yet when I dream awake, you are not there.

Must still I hear above the sunlight's clash,
your softer voice like fluting echo sigh,
and see the pinions of your spirit
flash on every drifting cloud the wind blows by.

In sleeping state I dream - and as I float,
Out-stepping time and over-spanning space,
I touch, I hold, I lean to you - and slow
My thirsty soul drinks in your beauteous grace;
Yet daydreams speed me from you fugitive -
You are not dead; but not for me you live.

MY FRIEND SYB

He didn't come to tell me off -
My Angel (dressed in green);
He came to bring a special gift,
A gift that is unseen.

He wrapped my gift in love and light
compassion, care, and lace;
and then he placed it lovingly
behind a smiling face.

He gave the gift to God to bless;
God held it in His arms,
and filled it to the brim with love,
tranquility, and calm.

And then he placed my special gift
within a heart so true,
a gift of friendship, fun, and love.
My special gift was you.

A DANCE TO DREAM

Somewhere beyond the Milky Way
where dreams are born with wings,
where snowflakes shimmer in the sun,
a fairy softly sings.

Somewhere nearby, yet far away
where love is spun from golds,
where Angels dance amongst our dreams,
a fairy-tale unfolds.

Somewhere out there beyond Sweet Earth
where snowflakes bright the dawn,
a fairy ring of love holds hands
with snowdrops on the lawn.

And somewhere, near a Tulip tree
where gold dust softly lies,
elfin folk and fairy-lets
embrace the soul that cries.

Deep in the midst, the Fairy Queen,
her heart a-soar with fear,
cups eyes in hands, her head bowed down,
reduced to mortal tears.

She grieves because man's cruelty
to planet Earth could sire
destruction in the hearts of those
whose Light would then expire.

Daunted when man fails to free
the blindfold 'round his soul,
seeks frail a path to percolate,
to heal, and blend him whole.

Her elfin courtiers ('twined in love),
circle dance in glee,
chiding her in cricket thrum
to set Man's blind sight free.

So silently, she gathers soft,
most cobwebs she can find;
To silk a woven web in lace
for love, and peaceful mind.

Dancing wide on tiptoed wing
of gossamer and lace,
spies Frost's mirror framed in smiles
that lights her lovely face.

Then as the sunlit-melted snow
soft-kissed her tears good-bye
the Fairy Queen, with hope-filled heart,
sang sweet her lullaby.

Her haunting words were echoed
by soft shadows on the run;
tinkling notes, so clear and pure;
"raindrops" in the sun.

Deep, deep within mans' Shangri-La
pulsating notes resound
and love, beyond Man's wildest dreams,
was felt and thus re-found.

And in that Land of celestial thrall,
where devas dance with dusk,
the Fairy Queen, her thirst anew,
quaffed dew from acorn husk.

She is Man's whisper in the wind,
A loving, flighted seed;
moon and stars a-dance with Angels
of a fairy creed.

As slow she sips, Man's thoughts alight,
Brimmed chalice spilling love;
'No more this blindfold 'round my soul -
"I think... I dream... I HAVE."

Somewhere beyond the Milky Way
where dreams ARE born on wings
where snowflakes shimmer in the sun,
a fairy softly sings...

US

I didn't believe I could feel this way
after all that's happened to me,
I never wanted to feel this way,
and I didn't want you to see.

You smile from your heart when you look at me,
and your smile dries my tears every time,
the depth of my feelings are very real
but my feelings don't count, you're not mine.

There are so many things I would love to say,
and so many words I could find,
but I'm frightened of telling you,
scared that you'll laugh,
for I know, deep, deep down that I'd mind.

If you were free now, I wonder just what
you would choose to do or to say,
and if you were free, just where would I be,
by your side, or some distance away?

My feelings are real, just like thoughts and
dreams
but I wish they would go away;
for the simple truth would be hard to accept
and you might not want me to say.

I love you, you see, my special friend,
but I'll never tell you so,
for you are committed, I understand that,
so you must never know.

70

WALKING THROUGH THE YEARS

Walking through the years, as I have,
blinded by the tears that I've shed,
helped me find all that I have.

    suddenly there's life
    maybe there's love
    always there's You.

Walking through fears that I felt,
working through feelings I had
helped me find all that I have

    suddenly there's life
    maybe there's love
    always there's You.

Knowing I walk with your Light in my heart
comforts me night and day,
and the healing of Angels that flock to my side
takes the pain of my past, away.

So take me I ask of You, take me to task.
Teach me to shine in Your Love;
hold me and guide me with wisdom and truth
held firm in a spiritual glove.

For You are the Love surpassing all need
a spiritual bower perfumed,
a cascade of gems sparkling with dew
spiritual flowers a-bloom.

The touch of Your Hands so gentle, so real
work hard to heal tired souls
lifting despair like a smile in the sun,
helping their destined goals.

71

SOUL HEALING

I came to you with mind outstretched,
seeking permission to serve;
but how could I know that before I would -
there'd be lessons I'd have to learn?

I came to you, with eyes shut tight,
but you smiled, and planted a kiss
upon the soul of one in need -
a soul no Love would miss.

You sent your Angels, framed in Light,
with my lessons, sealed in gold;
but you also blessed me with hope and faith,
and spiritual gems untold.

And then I felt you take my hands,
and I knew you were right there with me;
that together we'd give, the love from our hearts;
knowing soon, tired souls would be free.

So I held on tight, to faith, and trust;
and with reverence in my heart;
'cos in that moment - that second in time,
I knew my journey would start.

And now Father God; Divine Source of Life;
Essence of All, that is;
I offer my heart, and my mind; and my soul,
in service as long as I live.

SOULMATE

Hey you! Soul-mate! - quickly, grab my hand.
I'm sinking deeper and deeper into the black inky pit that is my
mind and I can't climb out -
I don't even think I want to.

It's warm, cosy and comfortable in here. I like it.
Here, I can find peace and quiet.
No-one can disturb me or make demands on me I can't and don't
want to fulfil.

I feel as though my life is floating by and I am watching it go -
helpless to chase after it and the "me" that once was.
I feel completely out-of control, shattered in little pieces, and very,
very withdrawn.
And yet I feel nothing.

Yesterday, a lifetime ago, I could remember the lush green fields of
my childhood and the peace I could almost hold in my hands.
I could certainly feel it.

Where has that magic gone?
If only I could recapture my strength of mind.
I need to be able to cope.

Please, please help me.

COLOUR ME BLUE

Cornfields of blue, yet not of corn,
bathed by the sun, in the sun,
rippling breezes fanning green leaves,
a blending of souls, one-to-one.

Spiders-legs petals of deep azure blue,
cobwebs of dew in cool morn,
waiting for daybreak to open it's eyes,
reflections of sun, spirit-born.

Nurtured by nature of God's precious seed,
unborn, immortal of man;
for Spirit's not born, so, cannot die.
It is, always was, always can.

Immersion of soul into cornflower head
inhaling deep, deep healing blue,
shimmers of sparkling silver and gold
reflecting the Light within you.

Hold that bright Light, your Spirit of Peace,
breathing its radiance within,
and then in the stillness thank God for his love
and forgiveness of mortal mans' sins.

CONFUSION

I forgive you.
For the hurt that I feel,
for the tears that I've shed,
for the pain that's engulfing my life.

I accept your rejection of my love.
I understand your reasons and wish you well.
But I hate you for breaking my heart.
Even tho' I forgive you.

In time I may be able to say your name.
In time I may be able to visualise your face.
In time, I may even be able to speak to you.
But not now, not yet.
Even tho' I forgive you.

I told God how I feel.
I told Him I thought you loved me.
But you didn't - I was wrong.

THE MESSAGE

Summer sand now weaned of wave,
and cleansed by moon and sun;
will herald birth of New Age shore
protected by 'someone'.

Sun and sky and bird on wing,
in soaring to the heights,
proclaims a freedom envied by
an earthbound spirit kite.

Man with spirit, soars like bird,
despairing depths, now low -
but man with spirit unaware
progresses long and slow.

Take nature's seed and blend with life
then nurture with goodwill;
the harvest reaped of man's intent
will serve to pleasure still.

Why doesn't Man now learn to share
the gifts from nature's hand?
Then seek to combine all he has
for use across the land.

HEARTACHE

All I ever wanted
was for you to hold me tight;
to feel your arms around my own
throughout those endless nights.

All I ever hoped for
was to feel your lips on mine;
to feel the warmth of silky skin
and not the hands of time.

And all I ever prayed for
was what we had -and shared;
a part of life I thought bereft
until our love we bared.

We took our love and held it tight
between two hearts, to blend;
a melting pot for dreams we shared,
a love no death can end.

But the the hands of time arrived
and carried you away
to start another life afresh,
a place where I can't stay.

I grieve for you, and want you back
not just in dreams alone,
so come to me and tell me that
my heart is still your home.

CHLOE

Trusting brown eyes spoke volumes
of the love we shared gladly with you,
of the walks in the park on the weekends
of the rabbits you chased in the dew.

You were more than a pet, darling Chloe
you were faithful, trusting, our friend
with a tail that never ceased wagging,
and ways that drove us round the bend!

For nine years of life, we enjoyed you -
nine full years, of mischief and fun
till one day we noticed your suffering
and knew God's will must be done.

Forgive us for ending your life, Chloe
but your torment was too hard to bear
and we couldn't go on just ignoring
the pain we all knew was there.

In the end, we then made the decision
to share you with freedom and peace
to revel in the love that you showed us
full-well knowing love cannot cease.

In spite of the guilt that still haunts us
we know our decision was right,
we know that forgiveness is ours now,
and we know that your love, is our right.

BELOVED

I kiss the tears that gently spill,
then glisten on your face,
I feel the ache within your heart
for love sent with God's grace;

I see the joy exuding from
your eyes of hazel-brown,
and then I sense the love within
so like a spiritual crown.

I watch the waves upon the sand
as slow they wax and wane,
I feel warm breezes bending boughs
of slender sapling canes.

I feel the sun, and see the moon
extend their light to earth,
and watch God's children play on sand
and laugh in joyous mirth.

Oh God of Love, teach me with grace
to learn humility,
to recognise that I am only
here to serve for Thee.

And in my serving, teach me now
to love my fellow man,
by sharing gifts within my soul
for use by those who can.

Then, in my loving, let me share
the joy that lies within,
with one beloved love I have,
immortal, without sin.

SOMEWHERE

Somewhere beyond the milky way
where dreams are born with wings,
where starlight dances in the dusk,
an Angel softly sings.

Somewhere beyond the moon and stars
where love holds hands with faith,
an Angel blows a healing kiss
upon a troubled face.

Somewhere out there, out-spanning time
where secrets softly sigh,
an Angel folds her wings round hope
and kisses pain good-bye.

Somewhere in time, where love is born
where moonbeams smile with care,
where soul-mates dance entwined in love
an Angel sings in prayer.

And somewhere, where you are right now
where Angels softly rest,
our souls can kiss and I can lay
my love upon your breast.

LIVING FLAME

Creator flame whose Light shines bright
within eternal soul,
compendium of All-Knowing God -
reveal our destined goal.

Eternal Source of Love, Light, Truth,
who dwells within our being,
release awareness with a smile,
that we may grow, all-seeing.

Touch now the flame that yearns within,
to grow eternally,
touch now the Light that seeks to shine
for all the world to see.

Touch now, our Spirit, rich in gold,
whose treasures we must seek.
Touch now the teachings you have taught
rejecting chaff from wheat.

Touch now the Living Flame that is,
whose aura blends with Thine,
touch now the Knowing in our souls
regressed no more by time.

Teach us, with love, Oh Inner Light
and with humility,
to find the God that lives within
if only we would see.

BUTTERFLIES AND HOLLYHOCKS

Butterflies and hollyhocks,
lavender and lace;
nasturtiums, poppies, marigolds,
honeycombs of grace;
cornflowers, daisies, dahlias, hydrangeas
pink, white, blue,
each waxy petal cast for life
by nature's spiritual hue.

Summer's waning, Autumn's born
those flowers will rest in peace,
until such time as Spring arrives,
and hibernations cease.
For that's the time fresh seeds will grow,
well-nurtured by the soil,
encouraged by God's wealth of mulch,
and mother nature's toil.

And so in life must we progress
along our stony path,
to rid our minds of discontent
and then our inward wrath;
It's up to us to light the lamp
of love, not dim it's flame,
and realise that healing hands
treat all of us the same.

I wonder if those caring hands
have helped you in your strife,
or maybe helped you realise
that God's part of your life.
Just as He helped the honey-bee
create his honeycomb,
so will He take you by the hand
and lead you safely home.

Summer's waning, Autumn's born -
The cycle cannot cease;
Just as the sandman casts his spell
And children sleep in peace.
So when your Angel blows a kiss
To let you know he's there,
Accept the love that comforts you
And thank him for God's care.

HEALING IS LOVE

The touch of Your hands, like gossamer,
the kiss of cobweb on lace,
the silk of a shroud that You beheld
the love showing on Your face.

I whispered silently "thank you,
for taking my hands in Yours,
for trusting me to do Your work,
for encouragement when I paused".

I know that You live in me
I thank You for my peace,
and I love You with all my heart -
a love no death can cease.

The need to belong to You
(a need we should not hide,)
the utter peace of going within
knowing You're by my side.

The warmth of the sun on an icicle,
the dew on a perfumed rose
the splash of a raindrop on a leaf
are You, to those who know.

A gentle caress of feelings
brought to the surface to heal;
chiding hurt and pain with love,
miracles that are real.

Radiant beams of sunlight
spilling into the dawn,
confirm that You are everywhere
that You are Spirit born.

84

LOWER SELF

I want to dance with Angels
soul-to-soul, on mystic wing;
I want to feel a breath of hope,
and hear a skylark sing.

I want to cleanse my Spirit
in frothy, foaming Might;
I want to catch a raindrop,
and hide it from your sight.

I want to kneel in prayer and love
to link the power within;
I want to feel my spirit soar
and hear the sunlight sing.

I want to breathe Eternal Light
and work in servitude;
I want to love and live again
and feel that love exude.

So, if you even DARE to think
that you can follow me;
my Higher Self, my guiding light
will heal and set you free.

LOVING YOU

$\mathfrak{I}$ see your smile, I feel your touch,
the greatness of your love,
I sense your presence in my heart
ambient from above.

Your touch is tender on my skin
my hair, or face, maybe,
I need your love dear spirit friend,
please call and comfort me.

In solitude I'm not alone
although I cannot see.
I know you're here, for thought alone
brings wings of joy to me.

And as I gaze deep, deep in mind,
I know just when you're near,
for colours glorious, myriad,
float by, dispelling fear.

So thank you Father for your love
ensconced within my soul,
I feel so humble in your arms,
but You will make me whole.

THE TRUTH

You are a snowdrop, crisp and white,
You are Jack Frost in dead of night,

You are springtime, yawning at dawn,
You are the summer, fresh as morn,

You are the autumn, green, gold and blue,
Now you are winter, bustling anew.

You are bare branches searching for sun,
You are the whisper of leaves, one-to-one;

You are a harvest of life and of earth,
You are creator of love and of mirth,

You are our life force, our prana, our need,
And you are within us, your wisdom to heed.

THE FAIRY GLADE

Incandescent bluebells
glistening in the sun,
crystal-toasted raindrops
bathing every one.

Fairy glades abounding
laughter ringing loud
Devas prancing merrily,
skipping round and round.

Woodland creatures curious,
gathering in a band,
wondering why their magic dell
is occupied by man.

Mortal man intruding -
eyes that cannot see,
ears that cannot hear the pitch
of fairy peals of glee.

Bowing elves to fairy gnomes,
merrily in dance,
daisy chains of fairy rings,

laughingly in stance.
Toadstool seats a-plenty,
respite for tired souls,
fairy wings of gossamer,
shimmering of gold.

Glistening threads of moonlight,
filtering through the trees,
sudden breath of silence -
all on bended knee.

Healing thoughts abundant,
ether-borne by love,
winging oft to weary souls,
Angels from above.

Woodland flowers bowing,
respecting those in need,
whispering words of comfort,
acknowledge fairy creed.

All God's creatures gathered,
Mammal, - bird - and tree,
holding hands with nature,
born of earthbound seed.

THE HEALER

He stood there - proud to be of Service.

The love in his heart was reflected in his hands through the purity
of his soul.

His eyes dimmed with the brightness of healing
as it emerged a thousand-fold in sparks of energy,
penetrating mortality in its search for the soul cause.

Here was the revelation - he was in tune with the infinite.
Completely. Utterly. Not with the ego of man, but with
humility towards the Powerhouse of Light
as eager to help as the one who sought.

The deed was done.

MESSAGE FOR MY SON

I cried for you my son
when you left home to bare your soul
and beat your fists against the savage breast of war.

I cried for you my son, in secret,
fearing I may never see you again this side of the veil,
and feel the terror of that knowledge knocking at my door.

I cried for you my son:
Product of my womb:
Too young to die, but not to kill:
and I would take your place.

I pray for all of you out there,
wearing crowns of courage that sparkle like jewels of light;
determinedly victorious against those sentinels of death,
flitting silently like a million fireflies dancing in the night.
I am frightened too.

I am proud of you my son,
who also shares the comradeship of war in lighter moments;
ever vigilant as sand in the sand in the desert sleeps.
So please, even in your darkest hour,
remember how much you are loved.

AN ANGEL ONLY LENT

As sure as daylight follows dusk
my love will follow you,
and all that I have I give you now
It's yours, it belongs to you.

Follow the stars and know I am there
to shine on your world - set you free;
'cos the pain and the grief that are now part of you
will be torn from your heart, by me.

The time that we had was complete for us both -
it was true, it was real, it was there;
so I want you to talk to me, tell me how it is,
I'll be listening, and I care.

I fell for your eyes, then your voice, then your heart,
'cos I saw all I needed there,
and the long years of searching finally went,
and I knew you were my cross to bear.

Take my love - all I give - all I have - for it's yours,
I love you, again and again,
do your work, don't give up, think of me where I am,
for I'm only next to thee.

So send your love to me, tonight,
don't ask me how or why.
I will hold it in my arms
and never say good bye.

WINGS

On wings we fly,

endorphic speed:

Where love prevails

there is no need

To weave and wind

along life's path -

Just heed the Universe's wrath.

SUMMER

Summer came and left in tears - not of sorrow but of joy.

She had done her best to bring sunshine upliftment into the hearts of the needy, but she was tired. It was time to go.

But in her fading a beautiful birth heralded a fresh awakening.

Autumn arrived; born in shades of gold that clothed her as a gilded lily.

What joy she brought into the life of Mother Nature as she tenderly enfolded her with a blanket of rainbow-burnished leaves, gently weaving a pattern of slumber on the rich humus of life.

She was so beautiful - a mantle of rustic reds and ambers, burnished coppers, and gold-tipped yellows sheltering the ebbing life of summer, seeking a mantle of warmth to shelter beneath before Jack Frost arrived.

In her coming a murmur of excitement jostled the undergrowth of the coming season - the change had begun!

AMY HARRIET

What do you see when you look at me,
You, now a hundred years old?
Gazing at me thro' old-fashioned frame
In clothes that were bought, then sold.

What do you see when you look at me
That begs to be understood?
Features that crept down the ladder of age
and a smile that would speak if it could.

What is the message conveyed in your eyes,
silently spoke from the grave?
May be the need to speak is not there;
Perhaps it's from alpha-wave.

Look at the ruffles around your chin
of gossamer and lace;
and 'round your neck a locket of gold
with ringlets framing your face.

Look in the mirror and watch your smile
Illumine eyes of blue;
Reflecting your warm and tranquil heart,
And aura of golden hue.

Amy Harriet, great grandmama, dear,
Thank you for being here!
Thank you for blending mind-to-mind
Via our spiritual sphere!

THE CAPTIVE

Who is this man
that has pierced open wide
the heart I am trying to seal?
Who entered my life
with a touch of his smile
and whose handsomeness makes me reel?

Who is this man,
with a beautiful soul,
whose eyes met mine a a glance;
Who is this man so modestly shy
but whose heart could lead me a dance.

A gypsy once told me that I'd meet a man -
(she 'saw' him in my hand)
a man who was honest and humble and proud
who would travel across the land.

She told me this man would enter my life
at a time when the sun shone on me,
at a time when my teardrops buried their grief,
at a time when I would be free.

My heart is now healing because of this man
who has entered my life as a friend,
a man who is special with no thought of self
a soul with whom I can blend.

If I can touch snowdrops for their wintry strength,
take comfort from sun, sea and sand,
Kiss autumn goodbye with hope in my heart
I'll know that God's work can be done.

And, if in the future, I'm meant to feel love,
to be part of its' beautiful might,
I'll know the 'Divine Source,' that 'Spirit of Love
Kept me safe, in its glorious sight.

JUST FOR A SECOND

Please - just for a second - hold me,
I need to feel I belong,
to lean my head on your shoulder
to fill my soul with sweet song.

Just for a second - hold me,
envelop me in your arms,
I miss the warmth of a beating heart
where safeness induces calm.

Just for a second - hold me,
let me cherish the warmth of your touch,
hold me, and kiss me, and love me,
for I need your loving so much.

Just for a second - hold me,
take mine - all I give - for a while;
respite for a soul that is aching,
a soul crying out, with a smile.

Then, just for a second - please let me
bury myself in your heart,
feel the strength from your life-blood exuding,
and knowledge that we'll never part.

MESSAGE FOR MY MASTER

You didn't see the dream we planned;
our castle in the air;
or if you did you held aloft
the plans we hoped to share.

You took without a second glance
the joy I thought was mine,
replacing it with crystal tears
that maimed the course of time.

How could you watch two lovers grow
then wrench apart their dream?
why couldn't you have turned your back
not set a tearful scene?

We didn't see what was in store;
perhaps our clouded eyes
concealed a truth that lay within
the heart that silent cried.

Fate took its course in iron-strong grip,
no mercy to lament.
did it not matter how I felt
or was death heaven-sent?

It felt so good, this love we shared
a love that cannot die.
A love for all Eternity -
a love for Steve and I.

WHISPERS OF GLORY

$\mathfrak{L}$isten in the morning
to the sea upon the sand,
Listen in the noon-day
to the flight of birds on land,

Listen in the evening
when the sun begins to set;
For everywhere upon God's earth
the needs of all are met.

Listen at the break of day
to linnets on the wing.
Listen in the summer heat
and hear a cuckoo sing,

Listen as the trees and flowers
speak soft amongst themselves
then listen to the voice within;
that whispers from the shelves.

MY PROMISE

I give you my heart
That you may open the door
And step inside.

I give you my Soul
That you may cherish that within
And allow the Light of my love
To fill you with spirituality.

I give you my trust
That you may always
Feel safe with me.

I give you my Truth
For I am I and You are You
Together we will share
ALL that Is.

I give you my thanks
For allowing me to be me
For accepting the person I am
Without judgment or trial.

I cannot give you my tears
For they were kissed by Angels
And no longer live in me.

I give you Peace
For my arms are a sanctuary
And when you are in need
I will be your refuge.

I give you Me
Knowing that you
Will love and cherish me
Until the end of time.

SPIRITUAL JOURNEY

Spirit touched your shoulders,
gently turned them round to see
a pair of eyes, translucent blue,
those eyes belonged to me.

You sensed despair deep in my heart,
deep-rooted, clothed in fear,
you felt my tears upon your chest
as then you held me near.

Through you I felt the love of God
reach deep within my soul,
I felt His healing power within,
to penetrate and flow.

And in that moment too soon past
I felt Him take my hand,
To tread life's pathway side-by-side,
He is the Promised Land.

FOR LOVE OF YOU

We forgot what we meant to each other
All those years, all those moments ago;
But I still love you now, more than ever,
And I still need to tell you, you know.

I still need to tell you I'm sorry
For breaking your heart when I did
I let other rule my emotions
Instead of just listening ad lib.

In spite of the years that have flown by
I feel you are searching for me
And when we have found each other
We'll know what our future will be.

Please don't be afraid that you've lost me
For I love you so much it's not true
And I'll always be here when you need me,
Just waiting, and wanting you.

So think of me now in your quiet time
Kiss my lips with your lovely warm smile
Put your arms round our memories and hug them
For we will meet again in a while.

Then when we're together, for ever
We'll blot out our tears and our pain,
We'll love one another in freedom
And be long lost soul-mates again.

THE GIFT

Loving is healing - so please hold my hands
let's walk through a future, golden of sand.
Thank you for bringing a smile to my face
when so many times I've fallen from grace.

Thank you for caring and loving and showing
the way that you feel - your smile is all-knowing;
I loved you a lifetime of seconds ago -
I love you this moment if you did but know.

Thank you for being so special to me,
for giving me space, and the time to be free;
loving is healing - a giving of self;
a combine of feelings brought down from the shelf.

Loving is special, invasive of heart -
forgiveness, and tears, a joyous fresh start;
loving spells caring, and hoping that life
will deal your cards kindly, discarding your strife.

Loving is selflessness, honesty, caring;
giving and taking, cherishing, sharing;
compassion for others desirous of need,
fulfilment of self:- nurtured of seed.

Loving IS healing; it's life and it's death -
a lifetime of moments, pure joy to caress.

SUNBURST

Love is like a flower
when sunburst dawns and smiles,
it's like a perfumed rosebed
that stretches out for miles.

Love is always with us,
bright-coloured like the sun,
its sepals and its petals,
reflecting spirit won.

Love can creep up on us,
its' stealth, quiet as the night,
invading lives with permanence -
a melody of might.

True love lives within us,
head bowed in reverence,
bringing joy and heartfelt smile
in every spiritual sense.

Love is like a rainbow,
sparkling jewels in the sun,
vibrating spiritual gems to earth,
soul-seeking, one-to-one.

Love is warm and tender
ethereal and free,
wanting, seeking, finding,
claiming you and me.

THE GLADE

Trees a-budding in the glade
where fairy gnomes abound,
magic mortals, spirit-winged
living oft above the ground.

Fairy dells a-ringing louder
heeding whispers from your world,
helping others needing guidance
from a spirit world unfurled.

Magic moments there-a-plenty
bringing joy to suffering souls,
washing sins and strife with love-soap,
helping man towards his goal.

Oh! the joy of righteous living,
keeping bright the path we tread,
knowing always, Love is with us,
guiding us in perfect stead.

LISA'S SMILE

Yours is the smile I see in the sun
on a lovely summer's morn,
Yours is the smile that lights up my life
like a wonderful breath of dawn;

Your smile is soft laughter that walks hand-in-hand
with the sun melting snow on the trees,
your smiles are like giggles that made me collapse
when you crawled on your hands and your knees.

Yours was the smile that broke my resolve
when I had to be firm with you,
Yours was the smile that brightened my day
like the sight of a cobweb on dew.

Yours is the smile that kisses sad lips
when you reach out with love in your heart,
And yours is the smile God holds in his hands
As he gives your young life it's fresh start.

Yours is the smile on gossamer wing
that soft breezes propel through the day,
Yours is the smile I remember at night
when the dusk whispers dawn's on its way.

Yours is the smile I hold in my arms
for the warmth and the comfort it brings,
For you my sweet child ARE A RAY OF BRIGHT LIGHT
from the haven of God's wings.

STARLIGHT

As crystal in a necklace,
as the fallen dew,
one facet, sparkling in the light,
reminds me, oh, of you.

How deep within that sparkle shines,
no thought for past remorse;
therein embedded in a throne
and woven from the Source.

Remember always that Bright Spark,
a Shining Star of LIGHT:
Hold deep that Light, unbound in grief,
and keep it in your sight.

Tomorrow, we should never look
towards in wonderment;
Today, and now, is all we have,
and it is Heaven sent.

Grasp your starlight in both hands;
FEEL a sense of pride;
Be still in Spirit, full of joy,
That Light shines from inside.

If I could reach out for a star
and give it straight to you,
omnipotence would would bow its head
in servitude to you.

BELIEVE

𝕱or all the times you've argued,
for all the laughs you've shared,
for all the years he's been your friend,
you know Dad always cared.

Time fades our pain, it doesn't heal
the sense of loss incurred,
but warm and tender memories
live on in us, un-blurred.

When death approaches those we love,
when life sits in the shade,
how desperately we long to cling
to sunny, childhood days.

For there we felt secure and warm,
and tears were kissed away
there, loving words chased far our fears
brought safety home to stay.

So now, whilst time is still your friend
let bygones rest in peace,
and let Dad know you love him still
that that, will never cease.

And when the sands of time run out;
when death knocks at his door,
know Dad will be with family
and let his spirit soar.

THE TRAVELLER

Blessed spirit, blood of life
who witness love supreme,
who stoops from heaven to earth below
to succour and redeem.

Breathe in our souls your breath divine,
grant us the grace to see
Your footsteps side-by-side with ours,
that we may walk with Thee.

Through all our sins, our griefs, our tears,
dear Saviour may we know
the joy of love, and cling to You
wherever we may go

And when we float on drifting cloud
in dreams out-stepping time,
our thirsty souls will drink Your grace,
to be forever Thine.

MY SPECIAL FRIEND

He is always with me - my God. We are one.

He is my heart, my soul, my consciousness, my self.

He is the air I breathe, the voice I am, the love I feel, the healing I give, the sun that shines after the rain.

He is the Cosmos, the dew on a rose.

He is me, and I am Him. He loves me, protects me, guides me, teaches me, reaches out to me.

He holds my hands when I stumble.

He IS the senses of the wild, the power of the horse, the attitude of man. He is my wisdom, my folly, my best friend.

He is my Higher Self.

DANCING WITH ANGELS

You can dance with Angels
aloft, on spirit wing;
You can hold the hands of joy
and hear a skylark sing.

You can dance with Angels,
their song already known,
Gifted are the wings of love
that cherish the unknown.

I was once an Angel,
in sunlight did I live,
now descended to your soul;
truth and knowledge give.

You are now that Angel
and you dance by our side;
You alone, regressed no more,
can free the hands of time.

You can dance with Angels -
and you, and you, and you!
Living, breathing Cosmic Light
within a special you.

Take the hands held out to you,
Grasp them in your might;
Then onwards step and falter not -
The truth is in your sight.

A GIFT FOR YOU

$\mathfrak{T}$ake what I offer you, the good Lord said:

> "An abundance of health"
> A wealth of prosperity
> and a lifetime's guidance.

THEN you will see how much I love you.

IF

Although I cannot see you
I know that you are near;
Although I cannot touch you
I know your love is here.

I want to hold you in my arms -
To share my Wedding Day;
But time and tide knocked at your door
And swept your lives away.

If Time HAD trod a different path
And fairy dreams came true,
They would have blessed the dream I had
To spend this day with you,

I need to thank you for the love
You gave unstintingly;
For teaching me that right from wrong
Allowed me to be free.

So long I've waited for this day -
To wed my man so true;
He'll cherish me, just as you taught,
And fill my life anew.

So can I thank you from my heart
WITH ALL MY LOVE ANEW
And will you hold God's hands for me
As then I say 'I do?'.

I GIVE YOU MY HEART

I give you my heart
That you may open the door
And step inside.

I give you my soul
That you may cherish that within
Allowing the light of your love
To fill me with your spirituality.

I give you my trust
That you may always feel safe with me.

I cannot give you my tears
for they were kissed by Angels
And no longer live in me.

Would you like my love?
For now and always?
That we may share
For the rest of our lives
The God-Light that resides within?

Then
I give you me
Knowing that you will love and cherish me
Until the end of time.

FORGET ME NOT

𝕴 am the dreamer and you are my dream,
You are the moonlight - I am your queen;
I'm trying so hard, to face reality
as death is the torchlight that searches for me.

Reality tells me that I cannot stay,
that the life we have planned will be taken away;
How can I leave you a love that's bereft
How will you cope with the pain that is left?

I love you so much, you are part of my life,
all I ever wanted, was to be, your wife;
I really believed that death couldn't be
the cruel, tireless friend I see smiling at me.

Sometimes I see angels with wings of pure white,
in gossamer gowns and hair shining bright,
there's one I recall who comes close to me
blue ribbon in hair and a smile just for me.

With a turn of my head I follow her gaze
and see in the distance a grey misty haze.
And when the mist clears, the angels in white
float gently away with a shroud, to the Light.

Please take me and hold me and love me tonight
before its too late and my strength fades from sight.
I know that my angel is calling for me,
that death is now cruelly beckoning me.

If I can just tell you that I will return
one day with a pink rose and feathered grey fern,
the love that they bring you will ease that dark pain,
and you will believe that we'll meet once again.

So hold me once more, my sweetheart, my life
before it's too late and your anguish is rife
'Cos my Angel in white is now calling for me,
To carry me home where my pain will fly free.

A COBWEB OF DREAMS

Sweet Spirit of Life, please help me, I pray,
to bathe in Ethereal Light;
teach me in whispers, on cosmic ray,
to blend with your rainbow of white.

Teach me to learn from my cobweb of dreams,
encompassing colours so bright
not even a vista of candles aflame
could extinguish its halo of light.

You gave me a colour, reflecting my soul -
Indigo, (deep purple -blue) -
for this is my essence of spiritual love;
I see it when I link with you.

You gave me Yellow, for knowledge and truth,
upliftment, and brightness, and fun;
for buttercup meadows, reflections on chins,
- the colour of sunshine and sun.

And then, after Yellow I saw Royal Blue,
and buried my face in its depth;
I inhaled its healing so pure in Your love,
derived comfort that dried tears I wept.

From Blue I sensed Orange, so vibrant alive,
I wanted to 'get up and go!'
It stirred inspiration, and I felt so good,
exalted , excited, aflow.

Then red stood beside me, companion in life
Giving strength when the going gets tough;
- A leader, a trouper, a rod and a staff,
I need it now, too, very much.

My pale apple Green is soothing and cool,
shades varied like spiritual broth,
a beautiful union of earth, sea and sky,
a blending - a marital troth.

And last but not least, sweet Spirit of Life
I thank you for violet hue,
For my cobweb of 'dreams' - my spiritual gems
Would not be complete, without you.

And so from the spectrum of life I have plucked,
a rainbow of colours for me,
each colour a strand from my cobweb of dreams
and shared so that others might see.

TEARS FROM THE HEART OF A MAN

Dear Father God, I have a friend,
who needs your help this night;
for he has lost a part of him,
his darling, precious, wife;

Please touch his heart with healing hands
and bless him with your love,
he needs to let his pain fly free,
released by wing of dove.

He wrote a letter to his wife
after that dreadful day,
to tell her how he felt inside -
so many things to say;

With tear-filled eyes, I read his thoughts,
brimful of love and care,
and he has asked that I read out
the words he wants to share...

.. "Yes, I really love you, although you've gone from sight,
and yes, I really miss you, especially at night,
but when I close my eyes and dream, I see you standing there,
happy, healthy, free from pain, forever in God's care.

Our love was special, we knew that, our friendship strong and true,
But we were lucky, blessed by God, and cherished all life through.
Remember all the laughs we shared in spite of all the tears?
Remember all the fun we had, in spite of silly fears?

Can you remember our first kiss, beside the garden gate,
then father yelling 'come on in, it's getting very late?'
Those magic moments make me smile, time after time again,
and for a second you are here, my lover and my friend.

You were the best friend I could have, for ever and a day,
And I will love you all my life, in spite of come what may;
I've prayed to God to take my pain and throw it far away,
I know that he'll do what he thinks best, whatever I might say.

..So goodnight darling - sweet, sweet, dreams,
I'll see you soon, I know,
Rest safe for me in your new home,
Beloved, of my own..."